I Spy with My Third Eye

I Spy with My Third Eye

Captured Truths of the Afterlife

A
TRUE
STORY!

KATIE E. BERYL

BALBOA.
PRESS

A DIVISION OF HAY HOUSE

Balboa Press books may be ordered through booksellers or by contacting:

Balboa Press
A Division of Hay House
1663 Liberty Drive
Bloomington, IN 47403
www.balboapress.com.au
1 (877) 407-4847

Print information available on the last page.

ISBN: 978-1-5043-0191-6 (sc)
ISBN: 978-1-5043-0192-3 (e)

Balboa Press rev. date: 04/11/2016

For those who believe, no proof is necessary.
For those who don't believe, no proof is possible.

Stuart Chase

I dedicate this book to all the people who find comfort, peace, and answers. May your spiritualism be your hope, faith, and guidance.

My story is true; I have only changed the names of people I write about. This is to protect their privacy and mine too.

PREFACE

Our little ears and excited hearts listened to my grandma's voice. She spoke softly about the future of a woman she once knew. We sat at the table bench with our special mugs, which held milky, watered-down tea and two teaspoons of sugar. We loved getting the beverage because Dad wouldn't allow children to drink tea, but Grandma would let us. We used those mugs every time we visited. My sisters, Anne and Gay, and I waited eagerly, sipping on our tea and listening to every word as my Grandma told of this person's future.

The reading took place in Grandma's kitchen in Portland, England, where her family lived. Betty was a stranger to my grandmother. My grandmother read Betty's tea leaves and told her that she would fall pregnant, but the baby would not survive. Betty scoffed at my grandmother. She said, "That is impossible." Betty told my grandmother that she was in her mid-forties and that she had not considered more children.

Months passed and then Grandmother had an unexpected encounter one day with Betty. Betty said, "You! You were right."

Grandma asked, "About what?

"Remember when you read my tea leaves?"

"Oh yes, I do."

"I did fall pregnant, but sadly, I had a stillborn." Grandma then decided she would never perform a reading ever again. Until …

When reading my book, please use highlighter pens. Different topics will be messages and have true meanings for you. You will need to reflect on them. At the back of the book are blank pages for your own notes. It will be your own personal reflection, leadership orientation, assessment forever!

MY VIEWPOINT

In the course of this book, I state more than a dozen times that spiritualism is not a religion. It is my utmost belief a higher power, other spirits, and energies walk with us. This platform is greater, wiser, and pure loving to us mere mortals. However, I do refer to this higher state as "God." I'm happy to put that label on this higher dynamism, this presence that overwhelms me with white light, makes me feel wonderful, and with which I have an unbreakable connection. I know and believe in my heart of hearts it's true to me. I can assure you that it doesn't mean anything more than that. And I'm not apologising for it either; I'm simply stating my personal view.

Your opinion of this will be just that—your opinion—nothing more or less.

CHAPTER 1

One should think about writing a book at least once in a lifetime. I knew that I would do this, but I didn't expect it to be about my psychic abilities.

When I was young, I always wanted something to happen. I remember asking a favour of God: "Please let me be able to see dead people." I had a fascination about the spirits and people who had passed over. I loved the thought of having the ability to communicate with those who passed to the other side. I also always had a fascination with Egypt. These feelings and emotions just grew and intensified as I got older.

My first encounter with death was with Uncle Harold, my grandmother's brother. I first met him when I went overseas with my grandparents, Alfred Kenneth and Katie Ellen May Wilkinson (nee Childs). They affectionately called each other Ken and May. I was only sixteen years old when I left Australia to visit our relations in England. We travelled all over England for seven months. We had interesting experiences that were full of life whilst I was there.

My uncle was a friendly fellow, and my grandma adored him. She respected and loved him but not his wife, Caville. She was, in my grandmother's opinion, nothing more than a gold-digger.

During our time in England, we stayed with Uncle Harold and Aunty Caville. They lived in Chickerell, Dorset in a lovely, semi-detached house with three bedrooms, two bathrooms, and a single garage. They catered to and looked after us well. Sometimes, we sat out in what they called their conservatory, a small hut with glass windows and a couple of deck chairs. On sunny winter days, it was nice to sit out there.

Chickerell was very different from where I lived; Brisbane, Australia, was always hot, and the humidity was high. We talked for hours in the conservatory, usually about the good old days. Grandma reminded me of things she and her brothers and sister would get up to. Grandma Wilkinson often talked about her family, especially about her parents, Edward Childs and Else May Brown. She loved them dearly. We sat and watched some television after dinner. Grandma offered tea, and we all accepted enthusiastically. Whilst sipping on our tea, we listened to Grandma tell us how on her father's side we were descended from Spanish gypsies.

Once I finished my tea, I'd ask my grandma to read my tea leaves. (When making a pot of tea, we always used loose tea leaves; I don't even think teabags were invented back then.) She always agreed; Grandma could never say no to me. Grandma also taught me how the read the future with playing cards. But she preferred reading tea leaves to any other method.

I finished my cup of tea quickly, impatient to hear what my future held. Grandma swished my tea leaves around in the cup, always three times, and then tipped the remains into the saucer. She analysed the cup with great awareness and in deep thought. She was always very serious when it came to this request.

Soon, she announced her findings. "Oh dear, you will be going to a funeral very soon."

"That's not good news," I said to her.

She showed me how the leaves had gathered in my cup. They were in a very even, straight line from the base of the cup to the very top lip of the cup. To me, it looked like a very long trail.

From my recollection, everyone in the house was asleep by 9:30 p.m. Later I awoke to strange sounds coming from my uncle and aunt's room and voices in the hallway. Then I heard my aunt shout for my uncle.

"Ken!" she yelled in a panic, "Something is wrong with Harold. His breathing is funny."

I leapt out of bed to discover that Uncle Harold was having a heart attack. Aunty Caville was hysterical. Everyone stood around helpless, watching him die. Grandad rang for an ambulance, but by the time the medics arrived, it was too late. Uncle Harold passed away in my grandma's arms.

We all attended his funeral the following week. He is sadly missed.

The day after the funeral, Grandma came to me. "Last night was the last time I'll ever read tea leaves." With that, she announced she was hanging up her psychic abilities forever. Caville passed away years later.

For many years after Uncle Harold's death, Grandma and I often spoke of the events of that terrible night. We wished there was more we could have done as he was dying. He was in excruciating pain and kept yelling out, "Stop the pain!"

My grandparents are deceased now. I miss them terribly every day. I remember the day Grandma passed away. I was in my early thirties. I went to her bedside at the hospital. She was fragile and pale, but she could still give me a smile when she spotted me at the end of her bed. Mum moved away from the bed so I could say goodbye to Grandma. She was breathing very slowly and wasn't able to talk. I leaned in close and told her I loved her. She said she loved me, too. I wasn't very brave; I began to cry. I couldn't just wait around for her to die. I told Mum and Dad that I was going home to my family. They promised to ring me and let me know when she had passed. Around 5:00 p.m. that day, I received the phone call from my dad, who let me know Grandma had passed away quietly.

To this day, I miss her. It's like a piece of my heart left with her. My dad told me what he experienced as she slowly slipped away. He said my grandma was troubled because she didn't want to leave us behind. Grandma told Dad that "they" wanted her to come with them, but she felt as if she was abandoning her family. Quietly and calmly, Dad reassured her it was okay to leave us and join her loved ones who had passed. She was an amazing woman, wife, mother, grandmother, and great-grandmother.

Just about every day, I've asked God if he would allow me to see things other people don't. Fortunately for me, I still get to connect with my loved ones anytime I want or need. You can have this same experience. Everyone has the ability. You just need to tap into your spiritual side, your psyche. Let go of all your built-up ego, and use your inner self to be your guide. Later, I will explain this in more detail.

CHAPTER 2

This is my journey. I became more in tune with my psychic ability at the age of forty-seven. Yes, I was that old when it finally happened. I still get excited when I think about this particular experience. I call it my epiphany.

My angel photo was taken June 27, 2009, at Port Arthur, Point Puer Island. This place was once a boys' prison; in fact, it was the first juvenile prison in the British Empire. I was on tour with a large group of people, and we were approximately 250 metres away. I saw a brilliant white light form what looked like an ornate cross and rooftop (the portal).

Figure 1-enlargement of original photograph

Arrows will help you identify various features of my photograph.

Figure: 7A

> Angel cradling an infant. At first sight and from a distance, it looked like an ornate cross.

Figure: 6B

> A young boy with dark hair; long, dark-brown pants; and shirt. He is crouching down and holds a portal. (From that distance this portal looked like the rooftop of a building)

Figure:5C

> Here we see three young boys. The one with blond hair and a striped shirt is in the middle. Do you see the dark-haired boy with a dark shirt on the right side? What about the other dark-haired boy on the left? There are others who stand behind them, too.

Figure:4D

> These are the spirit guides.

Figure:3E

> Another young boy, facing side-on, looks in the direction of the angel.

Figure:2F

> A dog, seated, is both watchful and protective.

This is the enlarged image of the original photo. Can you now see what I saw—an angel cradling a child?

Do you see the little boy holding the portal, crouching beside the tree?

Can you see the lost boys in the bushes to the left of the angel?

Can you see the other images of spirits reaching out to me in the photo?

This experience changed my life forever, and I hope it also has an impact on you. I saw it with my own eyes. I photographed it—my captured truth of the afterlife—with my own camera.It's all true!

There are so many more visions of spirits and apparitions within this photo. See if you can see them for yourself. Test yourself; try to connect with them. It's an amazing capability. I have the proof. I saw it with my own eyes, and there is no denying it.Let me tell you the story of how this all came about.

We arrived in Port Arthur on June 26, 2009. Michael and I were joined by Joanne and Stanley, and we stayed for two nights. It was a pretty place; quiet and peaceful. Michael and I love the surrounding and the areas so much. For some strange reason, we both feel like it's home.

We all went to the restaurant for dinner, and our ghost tour started at 8:15 p.m. the next evening. Our tour guide was Kenny. Earlier that day, we decided to take the cruise to the islands that were once part of the prison at Port Arthur. The first stop was Dead Man's Island. There were a lot of resting places of the dead from the 1800s to the 1900s. It was deemed as sacred land only after the Reverend George Eastman was laid to rest there. I ended up with one of the photos of a headstone with a few orbs surrounding it. It was very sombre as we strolled around the gravesites in the cemetery, listening to the tour guide tell us about the misfortunes of the convicts and the sad endings of staff and soldiers who once lived at Port Arthur.

Next stop was the island, Point Puer Island. This was where they housed boys who had been sentenced to jail. Boys as young as seven were sent to Port Arthur from England to be punished for their crimes. One young boy stole a toy and was sentenced to seven years in jail. The commandant at that time realised the boys needed to be separated from the men who were in prison. Hence, the boys were moved to Point Puer Island. Boys were taught trades such as carpentry, masonry, tailoring, and shoemaking and mending. This would be useful to them once they were released and reformed. At the very least, if they survived their sentences, they would be able to find a job.Can you imagine the hardship those young children had to face? Taken away from their families, jailed for years, and then expected to go and live a normal life once their time was up. This would have been positively unbearable and a very harsh existence. The government eventually closed the boys' prison and ordered the buildings to be dismantled and the stone shipped to the mainland for recycling at the main prison.On the last part of the tour, while we waited for the boat to take us back, the tour guide, Penny, told us about the church that once stood to the far side from where we were standing. Facing the jetty with the water in front of us, she pointed to my left. I turned to have a look and saw trees and bushes. I took another look. I could see a brilliant, white, ornate cross standing on the ground and what appeared to be a rooftop to its right.

I looked at it for a few seconds before asking in a soft voice, "Penny, sorry, excuse me. Is where that big cross stands where the church was once?" Penny kept talking about the tour. I thought, *she either didn't hear my question or she's ignoring me.* After a few minutes passed, I asked again, but louder. "Is that where the church stood—where that big, ornate cross stands, pointing in that direction?"

She replied, "I don't know of any cross."

I was pointing at the cross I saw and was pretty insistent about it. "I know what I am seeing."

Then Stanley, who was standing to the left of me, said, "Katie … what cross? I can't see any cross." I couldn't understand why he wasn't seeing it. It was such a brilliant, white colour. So white, in fact, it looked silverly white, which was luminescent.

Joanne and Michael, on my right side, asked me the same thing: "What are you talking about?" I still couldn't understand why they couldn't see what was in front of them. I bent down slightly and used my arm as a guide to pinpoint where the cross stood. But they still couldn't see it. It was then I pulled out my camera. "I'll take a photo of it to show you all it's there!" I lined up to take a photo. I could still see the image through the viewer, but Joanne still couldn't. Click … got the photo. There it was: a most breathtaking, brilliant, white cross amongst the bushes and what looked like the rooftop of the building.

I was so excited by this time. It was happening to me … what I had been asking for so many years. The spirits were putting me to the test, and I was over the moon. I didn't care if people chose not to believe me. I had a photo—my evidence—that there is an afterlife. I jumped for joy. People around me were shocked. Some were scared and moved away from me. Others embraced it and called me the "ghost whisperer." That moment in time validated my realism. The moment will stay with me until I die. The moment in time will be a timeless piece of evidence. My indubitably captured truth of my epiphany.

When I showed Penny the photo, she was gobsmacked. She called to the other tour guide, Kenny, to show the picture to him. Once we reached the mainland, we made our way past the reception area, where Joanne had mentioned to the girl behind the desk what I experienced. She, too, was amazed and without answers. She also called over fellow staff workers to look at the prize photo. She handed me a card with a woman's name on it. She would be grateful for a copy to put with the other unexplained photos. I decided I wouldn't be sharing that photo with anyone. But now I'm ready to show the world my captured truth.

As for the night tour I mentioned earlier, we had a nice time. I got loads of photos and saw so many orbs I couldn't count them all. Michael volunteered to be a lantern carrier for the tour, so everyone had to stay in front of us, which was great for me. I took dozens of photos. Towards the end of the tour, about the last twenty minutes, I saw the orbs right before my eyes. I could see the ectoplasm surrounding people in front of me and Stanley. I felt a sense of privy, for they all came out for me to see them. I could only hope they were at peace and not tormented. Touching the walls, doorknobs, and window latches only made me visualise the ones who used to walk these grounds and had passed. It was a very harsh life back in those days. This whole experience changed my life, my whole being. I had my captured truth, my wish, and my epiphany!Other photos taken by me are included in this book. They are real and miraculous!

What follows is Joanne's recollection of what she witnessed that day.

Near the end of the tour, the tour guide was telling us where the existing church had been at that time. She showed us drawings that were kept in a folder of what the building look liked and described them to us because there were no ruins or any remnants of any type of building. The buildings were all demolished years ago. Then the tour guide pointed over towards the trees in the distance. "This is where the church site was," the tour guide articulated.

Then Katie pointed and announced, "Is that where the cross is?"

Then I looked at Katie and asked, "What cross?"

Stanley, who was standing beside me, also turned back and said, "What's she talking about? There's no cross there."

Katie replied, "There, about 11:00 o'clock," using her arm and hand as a guide. So then Katie took out her camera and took a photograph of the cross. We both looked at the picture and said, "Shit, there is a cross."

CHAPTER 3

Michael and I made our way to Tassie, a prison site in Port Arthur, in 2008. There were old ruins and many old buildings to discover, and they also offered a ghost tour at night. Michael wasn't keen on the ghost tour. He said he wasn't going, but if I wanted to go then go. Yeah, right. As if I would go by myself. He was adamant in his decision. I was disappointed because it was something that was right up my alley and on my list of things to do.

Well, as it happened, at the place we were staying, the Fox & Dog Motel, there was a couple sitting at the bar whilst we, too, were having a drink before dinner. Their names were Missy and Redmond, a nice young couple from Melbourne. Michael had talked to them before I arrived at the bar. He said to me, "Katie, guess where they are going tonight?"

"I don't know," I responded.

They are going on the ghost tour at Port Arthur."

"Oh!" I said, smiling. "How wonderful that is!"

I told Missy how Michael was too chicken to go. Missy admitted, "So is Redmond. But we are still going. Why don't you come with us?"

"No," said Michael. Well, you know what I told Michael.

"Come on, come on, come on, and come with us!" They just didn't give up.

Before I knew it, the deed was done. The barman wrote out a bill for forty dollars and handed it to me before Michael could change his mind. We were going on our first ghost tour! Yippee! I was so excited.

Our departing time was at 8:30 p.m. on May 30, 2008, the day before my birthday. I couldn't wait; the excitement of maybe seeing something wouldn't leave my mind. I was so sure I would see a spirit/ghost, I had my faithful camera locked and loaded.

The tour guide, June, was very knowledgeable about the location and its history. She captured everyone's attention, especially mine. She had a few rules we needed to obey for our safety. Rule number 1 for politeness, there were to be no photos taken while she spoke. This was unfortunate because it didn't allow me to get as many photos as I would have liked. Oh, well, such is life!

However, the photos I did get were brilliant—better than I imagined. The feelings I had were indescribable. I felt a presence around me all the time; it was there especially at the large penitentiary building. I certainly felt an evil presence there too. I called them, using my third eye, to show themselves. I have proof in my photos that some listened and came forth.

My photos show orbs of energy, ghosts lights, and ectoplasm. What awesome sightings. One photo shows a distinct face. At that time, I didn't see it with my naked eye. I could only see it by using my camera and my mind's eye, where the energy was at the time. This particular photo was taken in what was called the dissection room. What was allowed to happen at Port Arthur back in the day was pretty gruesome.

Experiences with psychic cards and learning about the spiritual pathway from my grandma always had my attention. I knew that sometime, someday this would be an instrumental part of my life. I was never taught how to communicate to the spirits. It was only ever dabbled in every now and then because of my interest, curiosity, and excitement about the unknown. How blessed am I to have the ability to help others and to aid them in having more spiritual life paths?

My manifestation as someone who can talk to spirits may have taken many years to occur, however. I'm certain that seeing my epiphany, my angel, my young boys—whom all came out and let me witness to them—all happened when they were supposed to happen. There were times I second-guessed my ability, put doubt in my mind, and tried to convince myself this was just a dream. But the facts are here; it's the truth, and I've nothing to hide. Nor do I take my gifts for granted. I thank God and my angels every day.

It's important to listen with your eyes. The gestures shown to us, messages of hope, comforting words that embrace your heart and soul are amazing and quiet. Watch for the gifts from nature that are often shared. A singing bird, the perfectly coloured rainbow, rain, sunbeams, a child's laughter, and the roar of the ocean are all music to my ears and eyes.

Never pass up the opportunity to enjoy these great offerings. I began to write my thoughts down and also wrote poems about my feelings and emotions. I hope you can connect with them as I do.

Hello Friends

Hello, friends, glad you dropped in. I need you to listen; I need to tell you some things. I'm nothing without you, it is so true.

I feel sad that I treated you badly at times; why do you still tell me that love is blind?

We have been through so many struggles, you and I. I just don't understand why? Why I judge you and punish you and lie to you as well. Yet I turn around, and you are there with a smile.

You have been there through boyfriends, lovers, husband, and children. Sickness and it didn't matter; you guarded me from others, helping me be the person I am today. If it wasn't for you, there would be no me! Friends, you were there at my birth; you will be there at my death.

I promise to be great and try to be more honest and kind to you. Show you that I do love you and appreciate you, too. Kind and generous throughout the years left; body, mind, and soul who are one, it is me. I raise a glass and a toast to all three. Thank you, dear ones. I'll strive to be the best possible woman, my highest self.

Be Quiet

Sssshhhhh! Be quiet; don't utter a word.

Listen to your heartbeat and then you know you can be heard.

Close your eyes but not your ears; love will come flooding with levels filled.

Open your eyes, see all around; you have pictured your place, now begin the race.

Laugh with yourself. Never be afraid for you are not alone; the richness will be shared. Those around you will be washed over by your charms.

Dangle each charm, each bright soul, for that connection cannot be brought or sold.

Graceful pleasing, you remind yourself how fortunate you are that your pathway is golden; make sure there is no tarnish. There is no fear; this is the decider if you just listen and hear.

CHAPTER 4

T.I.M.I.N.G

Timing and acceptance can be same case scenarios, choices that are made. The emotions, feelings, and longings I felt were the same as an adult as they were when I was a child. The older I got, my feelings never really changed—only my appearance, like all of us.

Reflect on the how-

This book was written because I wanted to share my evidence and epiphany that God, angels, and our loved ones who walk with us throughout life are here with us on this earth.

We need to listen more and shut out the noise; turn off the right side of the brain that influences the lateral thinking. Common sense, reality, judgement, and self-doubt hinder speaking with the spirits. The biggest preventer that stops or cripples the ability to speak with spirits is the ego. You must let it go if you wanting that peace and unconditional connection on this plane.

Trust is a two-way street. There is always a beginning and an ending. The in-between elements are the modules. Trust one's self, and don't overthink things. The ability is there; you need to learn to tap into this tributary. There you will find the talent in your trust to find the answers to all the questions you set before yourself. It's up to you to decipher the meanings of the answers. Then ask your higher self which are the truths. So many times we confuse things by overthinking or believing it could be a trick. We do not understand the message (how we interpret it). Go with your gut instincts because your trust in yourself will never let you down.

Ask your loved ones who have passed over, angels, and spirits to show you how to bring out much-needed emotions. This sanctions us to reveal the inner beauty of the spirit presence.

Try not to allow the body to overcome the spirit or lose meaning. If this happens, you will miss out. You will find material possessions gaining more importance in your life. Stop reducing in human wants and feelings of entitlement over spiritualism. Let it wash over you. You should always strive to higher self-devotion in the spirit world and what it has to offer with a sense of knowing, love, and happiness to be shared with others. No tags or bias; just pure love.

Fake Is Fake

Take out the fake.

Take it out with the rubbish.

Don't let it clutter your life.

Fake is fake; don't be fooled

For it's never going to shine for you.

Let go of the fake.

Let go of its lies.

It was never a friend or supporter.

Take hold of your life; bury that past.

Aim straight and high—that's the goal; never respond
to the negative.

Fake is so second best.

Fake can cost so much and show no value.

Your worth is so much more.

Take back what is yours, and disregard the other once
that is done.

Look around, and see who's there; that's what matters.

Timing is everything. It was 1978, and I had just finished school. I
was sixteen, and I had two casual jobs. One was working at a snack bar
and the other a coffee shop. They were all right jobs, but I needed to
get one permanent job. I wanted to do hairdressing but couldn't get the

job. I didn't have a driver's licence, so I had to rely on Dad or my dad's relatives to take me to work. My parents wouldn't let me catch the bus.

My mother's parents were going to England because my grandma's mother had passed away. They had to sort out legal matters and receive her inheritance. Grandma suggested to my parents that they take me with them. I hesitated at first. But Grandma talked me around, telling me I would have the time of my life. It was agreed that I would go with them. In March 1979, we would depart and return the following September.

My expenses were taken care of, so all I needed was spending money. Dad agreed he would give me a dollar for every dollar I saved to use as spending money. I saved $300. He paid up, but thinking about it now, it must have been a massive chunk out of their savings. Back then, family finances were never discussed with the children. It was a no-go area. By the time I converted $600 into pounds sterling, I only had 300 pounds. My mother made me a suit. She is very clever like that. She can turn her hand to just about everything and anything. It was dark brown, and I had a beautiful floral, silky blouse underneath. My shoes were beige, high-heeled slides. I felt so grown up.

Grandma gave me one of her coats. It was a creamy, off-white colour. I hated it. It reminded me of an old detective's coat from a bad movie. It wasn't stylish enough for me. Grandma told me I would be glad of that coat when we arrived at Heathrow Airport. No way was I wearing that coat. I thought maybe I could leave it on the plane. Hmmm.

We could feel the cold creeping in through the walls of the plane. It was freezing. As we got off the plane at Heathrow … you guessed it. That ugly coat became my best friend.

Who would have known that we all would be attending a funeral in only two weeks?

After arriving back in Australia in September, and sporting a different hair style, figure, and pommy accent, I needed to get a job. I applied for a job in the shoe department at large department store at Cannon Hill. I got the job and was so pleased. I loved shoes and still do. They are my Achilles heel! Pun intended.

After being at the store for approximately six months, I was transferred to another store. It was great because it was a new store in Capalaba, which was closer to where I lived.

At this stage, I was dating a guy named Leo, and we became engaged. We were together for just over two years before I broke it off. In the end, Leo was not who I thought he was. We had different ideas, and I knew we would never be on the same page.

This was my life-altering moment. I met my future husband and love of my life at work. Michael was my boss. He was actually engaged to someone else at that time, and I was still engaged to Leo. I was offered a job in the sporting department in the store... I almost decided not to take the job. Since I was not a male, I was overlooked for a manager's position. And the guy who was the manager was a creep towards the women on staff. Back in those days, we had to put up with harassment from men. I also worked Thursday nights at a hair salon, trying to break into that industry.

After working in sporting department for about six months, I was offered a manager's position. I loved it. This was around November 1981.

Michael's engagement fell through, and he was living back with his brothers. His father had passed away in February 1981.

Unbeknown to both of us, it was the start to our love affair. Things were just awful between Leo and me. We had fights, arguments, and downright nastiness. We decided to postpone the wedding. I wish I had listened to the voice in my head. But I continued our relationship, knowing he was not the right man for me.

It was Christmas, and there was going to be a work Christmas party at Colmslie Tavern. I was eighteen years old, and I had never really been out like that before. I was always accountable for where and who I was with when it came to Leo. It's weird how you can be blindsided when it comes to the people in your life. You take it for granted that they will always want the best for you. But he treated me like a possession; I just didn't realise it at the time. Leo put me down in front of friends and his family. It made him feel like a man and that he was in control. I suppose I did live in a fairy-tale world, looking for my prince. He was to take care of me, and we would live happily ever after. This is what we were taught at a very young age. I was so naive.

At the Christmas party I had the time of my life. My friends from work were glad that I went. Michael was glad to see me. (I was glad to see him as well.) We talked all night. I didn't want it to end, but it did. I asked him if he'd like a ride home. I hadn't been drinking. He said that would be great.

I dropped him off at the end of his driveway. He got out of the car, stuck his head though the driver's side window, and thanked me for the lift. I wanted him to embrace and kiss me. But he was a gentleman, and I was still engaged to Leo.

I knew my heart of hearts it was the end of my relationship with Leo. I would have to tell him it was over. I arrived at his parents' house to a not so good welcome. Leo yelled at me, "Where have you been? It's late. Who have you been with? I rang your father because I didn't know what to think. Your father is on his way to my house."

I lied to him, saying that I left the tavern at ten. The problem with that was it was now just after eleven o'clock. I couldn't tell him I drove Michael home. Leo started calling me names. His parents were in on it as well. They were enjoying my misery and with any opportunity, stuck their two cents worth in—especially his mother. Looking back on it now as a parent myself, I suppose they were supporting and standing by their son like all good parents do.

I just couldn't take it anymore. I got a grasp of my engagement ring and quickly pulled it off my finger. I handed the ring back to him. I told him, "That is it. I can't marry you," and walked away.

Dad waited for me in the car once he arrived at Leo's house. I walked up to the car and opened the door and got in, we drove off and we made our way home. I think he was more upset that I left Leo. He kept saying, "What have you done? You are stupid for giving up on him."

That next Monday morning I announced to everyone at work that I was no longer engaged. I was happy. A huge weight had been lifted off my heart.

Leo tried to win me back with promises of things and to be more understanding, but I saw through that. Besides, Michael was someone I wanted to get to know better. I could feel a strong connection with him, as he did too. After a few weeks, just before Christmas Day, Michael asked me out. Would you believe we played games of court squash? Nothing else was open because it was Christmas Eve.

We were inseparable from that time. He asked me to marry him eight weeks from our first date, and I said yes. Michael was the person I had waited for all my life. The wedding was on the May 15, 1982.

It was a beautiful wedding. A lot of people didn't think our marriage would last, but we have celebrated thirty-three years of marriage and have three magnificent and wonderful children. Well, I still think of them as my babies though they are adults.

I always felt someone whispering answers into my head. Sometimes I listened and other times not. That's free will, which God gave to all of us. It's our right to choose what path we take. Whether that turned out to be the correct one or not, it was our choice. Timing had everything to with this time of my life's journey as it is in our everyday lives. We need to pay more attention to the messages and guidance given to us.

CHAPTER 5

It was 1984, and Michael and I had been married for about two years. I joined a ten-pin bowling team at the Greenslopes. My aunty asked if I'd be interested in joining. We had just moved back from Toowoomba to Brisbane. Michael had been transferred to Toowoomba from Capalaba. Toowoomba was a country town and lacked city conveniences. We didn't really like the place and was glad to transfer back to Brisbane.

I wasn't working at all. I needed to do something, so I decided to join. We met Thursday mornings. It was a great social event, I got to meet a new group of people. All quite nice. I was allocated to another team because there weren't any spare places on my aunt's team. The girls on my new team were lovely. They were very gracious and made me feel welcome.

After weeks passed, I sensed there was something happening with one of my team players. Her name was Lyn. She was whispering to one of the other girls and were making faces at each other. I decided to ask Lyn what was she experiencing that took her mind off the game.

Lyn divulged that she could contact the dead. They spoke to her through pen and paper. She would write, write, and write, but she wasn't the one moving her hand. Lyn said she had gone to a psychic who told her a French man was trying to connect with her. He did know of her in a past life. Lyn didn't tell the psychic about the writing, which was in French. Lyn didn't know any French.

I was amazed and very jealous. I would love to be able to contact someone who passed over. I tried it, and I did get something. Her name was Edie. When I think back about why it didn't develop into anything, I see it was because my ego. My huge ego.

Egos are weird things. You can be blindsided by your ego or feel excited, as I did. I was so excited because I just couldn't believe it chose me. And then I bragged about it to everyone. I was losing sight of the message they were sending me. I was the one—not God, angels, or spirits—preventing things from happening. It was only me and my damn ego.

I didn't have the right kind of guidance in that area. This was a missed opportunity to speak with the spirits. In other words, if I had the right vision, mindset, and more spiritual direction, maybe things would of been different. Then again, I am a firm believer, and my motto is whatever happens in life, whether good or bad, is meant to be. I have said and believed that from a young age. Yes, it was hard at times believing that when something didn't go the way I wanted it to. I would question myself, "Why me? Why is this happening to me or my family." The real question is, if you didn't go through your hardships or accomplishments, would you be the same person you are at this very moment? I don't think so. I have learned these are tests given to us. These are life lessons to bring us closer to God and to make this a more loving and peaceful planet. These lessons are to enrich our love for our loved ones and friends and to have an awesome life. It has certainly taken me a long time to listen to God and his angels. But now I have a more precise view of what I need to achieve before I die and how to do so.

Age never feels any different as you grow older. Sure, we show aging through our body with wrinkles and other signs of aging. Some people show it more than others. This depends on our lifestyles and whether we have taken care of our bodies when we were younger. But my mindset is the same as I remember it was in my late teens and early twenties. The only thing that has changed is I now have wisdom and a stronger belief in the afterlife, God, angels, and all those who have helped me along my life path. The lessons and purposes of our life bring the wisdom that has cradled us from birth. I believe the best things in life are when you have had an impact or inspired someone else's life, and you aren't aware of it. It means you have been given an opportunity to share your soul without ego, payment, or non-reciprocal gestures. There is pure gratitude in helping others through a genuine heart and love and faith.

Try not to premeditate your goodwill. Goodwill cannot be calculated, so it cannot be brought or sold. However, it is a valuable commodity in a person's character/disposition.

CHAPTER 6

Understanding self-esteem and being able to apply in your daily life can be tricky. Hence, don't listen to what others say about how you should either act, think, or pursue. Self-esteem is a foundation of what you know about yourself and then project to others. Self-esteem is a true gift.

This can make some people very anxious. The only way others can take away your feeling of good self-esteem is to judge you and be critical of you. This, in turn, makes them feel good and justified. Absorb the applause and accolades of your peers, family, and friends. If you ever find yourself lacking self-esteem, please don't listen to others. They have their own issues, and they have nothing to do with you.

So start looking in the mirror. It's a great beginning. Try to see all the things other people see. Tell yourself you are glad that you are you. Today is a new day; surround yourself with people who love and care about you. I bet that there will be a slight grin on your wonderful face. This was aha moment for me.

> Self-esteem comes from being able to define the world on your terms and refusing to abide by the judgements of others.

We sometimes have to trust in our instincts. Instincts are the essence of apprehending the interruptions of our life guides. If we choose not to follow these instructions or messages, the outcome might be the same. However, the pathway may have different consequences. Therefore, what is learned may not be the focal point of the lesson. It may be the missed opportunities—the ones you prayed for—or the answers and help from the angels and passed loved ones you need to help guide your life and to live it to the fullest. Don't waste valuable time and effort on relationships, for example, that could have been or that unfolded to be something other than what you thought they were.

I believe those people and relationships were only there for a short time in your quest of life. Ask yourself if you learned a lesson from this. If you didn't learn anything from this lesson (this breakdown of a friendship or relationship), it wasn't meant to be your lesson. It was the other person who needed to learn. What happens from that is not your concern.

That is why the ideal is to realize the value of the lesson and apply it as you go forward on your journey in life. Sometimes you may feel that you are making the same decisions again and again. Don't be fooled by people and their excuses. Have a direction, and the rest will come if you know in your own mind you did your best and are the best at what you do. That's also the magic in life—applying. If one can do that constantly throughout life, imagine the ripple effect it will have on others. Not only would you be gratifying your existence but that of others as well. But instead of being filled with all the passion and purpose that enable us to offer our best to the world, we empty ourselves in an effort to silence our critics.

Never Judge Anyone

And let no one judge you. No one can understand what you are going through unless they walk in your shoes. No one can understand the storms you have steered through, what battles you have fought quietly, or the scars you carry inside your heart. Believe in yourself, and cherish the people who uplift, encourage, and motivate you. Even those who challenge us the most can be our greatest teachers. They are the ones who sometimes shake us into stepping out of our comfort zones to grow and find the courage to stand up for our self. They make us realize we need to believe in ourselves and our self-worth and find new beginnings.

Have hope and have faith in your journey.

Good things are coming your way.

Just because things are stormy now doesn't mean you aren't headed for sunshine.

Have faith. Be strong … and never give up: the law of attraction.

No matter how far you have gone on the wrong road, turn back.

It doesn't matter how much time, money, or energy you've already invested in the path you've chosen, it's never too late to change direction when you believe your instincts are telling you to do so.

Always follow your pathways in life, as you are doing. Stay strong, and your trust in yourself will determine your ability to accomplish amazing things.

Feeling stuck or unhappy? You can change that! Too many people believe themselves to be too far gone, too old, or even too successful to choose a different, more joyful path for themselves. This is never the case.

Each day and each moment is a clean slate. Forget what's come before, and don't waste time worrying about what might or might not come. Here and now are what's important.

So ask yourself if everything leading to this moment was wiped clean, would I still want to be where I am right now? If the answer is no, you know what you have to do. Be brave. Take each day as a fresh start, and do what needs to be done to make you happy now.

Meditate; it's like an electricity boost for the soul. It also manufactures regeneration for the mind and body. Meditation is like a search engine to find your loved ones who have passed over, answers to your questions, and peace, serene congruence that can guide you on your pathway of life.

This is quite amazing when you think about it. It's like your special iPhone link to past, present, and future, and copious amounts of gifts.

Yes, our beloved ones who have passed over are still with us. They are minders to us all here on earth. There is no suffering where they reside. They are more than willing to help us when we ask for it. They are there to help us alleviate our load when everything else might be unsuccessful or if you need help to watch over your child or someone you care about deeply. How many times can you ask for angels and spirits to help you? They are always by your side to help you until the spirit leaves the body through death.

Sometimes it can feel like forever when waiting for help. Keep in mind the objectives can be right in front of you. Look for messages being sent to you. You need to be proactive at the same time, using your education, trust, inner being, and faith to help you achieve your goals and dreams. It's like steering a ship. If you steer the ship on the right course but there is a storm or rough waters, you can rely on sonar equipment to provide signals to guide you on a safe passage. Same goes for a more spiritual life. Opportunities will arise. People come and go in your life every day. Some will help you. and others will stress you. Just ride them out and wait for the life raft.

Our spiritual guides can protect and shield those with willing hearts. But they will never interfere with someone's pathway in life. They also have boundaries they must adhere to. Your life guides, God, angels, and spirits all work together and with each other.

You see why you should never feel like you're alone. Someone is always walking with and beside you with a steady, guiding hand.

Meditation—Surrounding Yourself with the Angels

This can be read out loud by another person, so the one going into meditation can be relaxed and enjoy his or her journey without disruption. Read slowly—take your time—as you both can benefit from a platform of communication with spirits and guides.

Sitting in your favourite chair, position yourself with your feet firmly on the ground. Or you can lie on a bed or in reclining chair. Just make sure you are comfortable, and there are no distractions such as TV, radios, people in close proximity, pets, and children.

Close your eyes, and let your muscles start to relax. Start with the tips of your toes and then to your feet, legs, back, and your shoulders. Let them release any tension and stress. Relax your neck and your head. Do this very slowly. Don't be in a rush. Take your time to feel and embrace the passageway to the beyond.

Breathe in through your nose and out through your mouth. Take long, deep breaths, so you fill your lungs to capacity. Blow out to empty your lungs. When you breathe in, I want you to imagine positive signs floating around you in the air. I want you to suck them in with your breath, and deposit these positive signs throughout your body. When exhaling, visualize negative signs racing throughout your body. As you exhale, I want you to vacuum up those negative signs and expel outward with your breath. Repeat this several times, until you see and feel only positive signs within your body.

Once you are relaxed, drift off and imagine yourself in a landscape of the lushest, greenest, grassiest meadow you've ever seen.

You see a gate. The gate is made of heavy old timber. There are markings on the gate. You can make sense of what is written. Feel how worn the gate is. Look for the catch that opens the gate.

Lift the catch, and walk inside the paddock. You see it's filled with beautiful wildflowers of all different colours. Visualize birds flying overhead and the smell of country air.

Feel the grass under your feet. It's cool, soft foliage brush under the arches of your bare feet.

You feel so relaxed that you decide to sit down on the grass. You detect a slight summer breeze caress your cheek. Closing your eyes, deeply breathe in the fresh, clean country air.

When you exhale, open your eyes and become aware of something in the distance. It's too far away to see what it is clearly. The breeze tosses your hair out of your eyes, and you can see distinctly what's in the distance.

You can see a white light, a light so white it gives you an overwhelming sense of love and peace. You stand up to move closer to the light. The closer you get to the light, what it is becomes more apparent.

You see large wings and a loving and kind angelic face. The angel calls you by name; you draw closer. It's then the angel envelopes you in its wings and sends even more white light to you. You feel safe and protected. The angel has come to take you on a journey of enlightenments. The truths are for you; listen to your angel with your heart for every heartbeat comes with loving guidance. Go with your angel now.

This is when the reader needs to be silent and allow the meditator to go into astral travel. To begin, set a time of ten minutes—or longer or less if you want, there are no rules. Once that time is up, you can slowly introduce the meditator back into earthly time by using a quiet voice. Say, "It's time to come back [the person's name here]. Say thank you to your angel, and give thanks to those who came through for you this day. Wish them well and a safe journey home. When you are ready, open your eyes and feel the afterglow and serenity."

Then you may want to discuss with your reader your experiences when you astral travelled. It's completely up you how to proceed with this; it's an individual discussion for everyone. There is no wrong way or right way; it's all to do with practice.

You can always check to make sure your chakras are well balanced, too. Understanding and activating the body's seven main energy centres is a must. The chakras are not in the physical body; you can only fix them through meditation.

The colours are

Red—base/root chakra

Orange—navel chakra

Yellow—solar plexus chakra

Green—heart chakra

Blue—throat chakra

Indigo—third-eye chakra

Purple—crown chakra

White light—a higher self

Everyone needs to do astral travel on a regular basis. It usually happens in a sleep state of mind but can also happen in a daydream state or meditation state. It happens when the spirit moves away from the physical body. There is more about this in the next chapters.

CHAPTER 7

Giving to others can make you happy and feel good as long as you're doing it for the right reasons and not because you feel less valued as a person, are a people-pleaser, or you're putting your own happiness at risk.

Why is it that people always ask, "When is it my turn?" What a load of crap! Most likely they are the type of people who rely on others to make them happy. So get off this perpetual merry-go-round if you are one of these people. If you don't, you'll never find your true, fulfilled happiness from within.

Would you suggest that there are levels of happiness within your life? It takes a lot more energy and a focused mind, to want to be happy. However, what measures do you put yourselves under? How happy is happy? What would you say if you were asked this question?

This is my understanding on happiness. Happiness should not be measured; it should always be like a constant smile. Happiness is an attitude, and we can make it a reality in our life if we choose.

Chase away all materialistic values, and begin to gather all the happiness in your life. Listen to yourself speak and your thoughts telling you what you have. Feel the thoughts as well.

Question and analyse everything you consider happiness.

You will be surprised by the outcome if you are truly honest with yourself.

Why do people reserve happiness? It should be the first feeling of the day.

"Why?" you ask. It's a new day full of hope and new beginnings.

Why bring yesterday's woes with you into the new day?

I'll tell you why. Habits and laziness! These two effects are mind-numbing and easy to settle for. It seems we have no problem being unkind to ourselves and putting ourselves down. We don't consider us not worthy of listening to our inner selves.

Why is it when we don't feed our inner selves, but at that moment we can demonstration our exterior selves in a complete contradictory manner? Good question.

It's called hidden light/soul created pleaser. It's you who is doing this to yourself. It's not anyone else's job to change this behaviour but your own.

Happiness shouldn't have a use-by date. It should always be valid and a given in our souls and hearts.

Happiness can be shared, but be sure you are sharing it with a true heart. Trying to be a better person is so much harder however, the rewards are far greater. This is where a lot of us fail. It's okay to fail. It's not okay to not want to try again.

To have extreme heights of individualism is a rarity. Strive each day to better yourself. Look at each day as an achievement and a new chapter of life lessons. This will validate the happiness mode you have created each day, making it brighter, stronger, and enough for you and for you to share and spread your happiness freely without wanting or needing anything in return.

Being Humble

What's that?

Being humble is a true reaction to a feeling you have. It's what you stand for and allows others to judge you based on your behaviour. It's marked by meekness or modesty in your behaviour, attitude, or spirit. It's not your arrogance or prideful self. Being humble allows you to feel empathy and compassion towards others. It is a unique emotion and shows gratitude.

To have a humble approach requires there to be no ego or to show pride or arrogance. Being humble needs to show there is no agenda, pride, no emotional thought process. One is seen as pure, unassuming, and sometimes shy. It's okay because it comes from a good place—a loving and giving heart.

Please don't confuse being humble with politeness. Politeness is the practical application of good manners or etiquette. It is a culturally defined phenomenon, and, therefore, showing this towards others and observing accepted social graces are skills but far from being the same as humbleness.

As you use your inner feelings and clarity, trust in your intuitive self's abilities. This allows you to guide your intuition in your everyday life.

CHAPTER 8

Comfort Zones

You need to be able to identify what is fear and what is comfort. Comfort zones are boundaries one creates around his or her earthly life. You feel at ease and shielded in comfort zones. They provide a sanctuary and provide no expectations or thoughts. They happen instinctively. Comfort zones deliver mediocrity. They won't fail you or break any rules. These zones create a buffer with nothing beyond. You are living with a barrier nothing can penetrate inwards or outwards. It's like being in mid-suspension.

If that's your mindset, maybe you want more. Do you find yourself thinking, *Gee, I don't think things can change for me I'm doomed to be only a certain way, feel certain things, or behave a certain way*? I'm here to tell you no. You can change things if you really want to.

For you to be able to acquire new things or to learn and educate yourself more or to be able to get more out of life no matter your age, you need to push those barriers and comfort zones forward. Push them until they are out of your reach. Only after you have accomplished this series of concrete actions will new escapades, people, places, and memories be unleashed into your life's path. You need to make the change and find the new momentum in your life. Create something tremendous in life, and keep on track. Don't fall back into mediocrities. You are accountable to yourself; that is no one job but your own.

It doesn't matter how big or small the change. The point is to acknowledge to yourself that you are too much in the zone and need to make and create a shift.

So many people I've spoken to are in a state of depression; aloneness; separation anxiety; anxiety; addictions, including drugs, gambling, eating disorders; self-loathing, judgemental personas; broken homes; are abusers; and haters who don't realize they are just that—bullies. Yes, it takes guts, a strong will, a positive mindset, conviction, the right edification, principles, and self-loving to make a change. But it can be done!

No More Excuses!

"Excuses" and "buts": these two words are used all the time when providing a reason as to why we don't take on new, inventive ways to transform our lives. What holds us back?

This is most definitely a case of fear, laziness, or both. To make a change in one's life is to create something new. I can't make it any clearer than that. You make the change. It's up to you to break through those walls, an interception of transparency, if you like, will lift you higher within your inner self. Serotonin levels and endorphins are released from the brain, so you have that feeling of overwhelming awesomeness. Hence, self-loathing will start to fade and extra white light will be redirected towards and become attached to you. Embrace the change. Share the prominence with your friends and family—even strangers. It's the ripple effect again. It just may be that on the day you happened to share your story about the thing that changed your life forever, you inspired someone to do the same thing. How wonderful is that? That is what I call a revolution.

My comfort zone was making me stagnate. I didn't believe it was making me miss out on life lessons, memories, experiences, and so on. But I was missing out on life. I had gifts, life's treasures given to me, and I wasted them on my fear of heights.

I allowed my fear of heights to devalue my life. So many times I tried to conquer it when I was younger, but I failed miserably. It was only when I understood the why—why I had a fear, my lack of understanding it, and how it became a handicap in my life—that I was able to deal with it. I also suffered with severe motion sickness. I related the two issues as one problem. For years I blamed my fear and comfort zones for saying no to any opportunities that heights or the possibility of motion sickness. I'm scared, I'm frightened, and I'm going to vomit!

So I missed out on many helicopter rides in different countries. In New Zealand I missed out on the experience of flying and landing on top of one of the mountains and not see the fresh, crisp, whitest snow. Not to be able to run, walk, lie in the snow, or see the surrounding landscape. I don't have that memory; I can only imagine.

In Hawaii I didn't get to experience up close one of the prettiest, most beautiful waterfalls and landscapes the island has to offer. Or to see the burst of bluest blue waters from above. I don't have that memory; I can only imagine.

In San Francisco I didn't get to experience the wonders that old city has to offer me—to take a ride and fly under the Golden Gate Bridge or see Alcatraz from above. I don't have that memory; I can only imagine.

So who was to blame for this?

Was it my fear?

Who stopped me from experiencing these things?

Me, not fear!

I created the fear; fear didn't create me. I created the solution to fit the fear in my own mindset. Do you see the pattern?

- Create
- Solution

- Fear
- Mindset

I have missed opportunities, and I have regrets for every one of them. I'm kicking myself that I didn't push and go outside my comfort zones. I convinced myself it was right not to make new memories, not share, and not to grow or learn or educate myself.

However, I have made changes in my life practices. What? I'm taking my own advice and stared down my adversity—my fear of heights.

Make a decision to change.

- Create to change.
- Resolve to be inspired and to inspire.
- No more fear; new memories accumulate worth.
- Mindset change means it's your contract to change; it's no one else's assignment.

I'm happy to share with you I pushed myself while travelling to Singapore in 2015. I'm so grateful for the chance to ride in the cable car. I pushed through my barriers and walls, and I inspired my friend to do the same. As I mention earlier, it doesn't matter how big or small the step you take. That step is the substance. It changed my life. I met people and saw things that will be detailed in my thoughts forever. I'm choosing the helicopter ride if the opportunity presents itself next time. No more missed memories or inspirations. If you're inspired by my leap of faith, I'm so happy for you. You can do it! Believe in your mindset change, trust that your life guides are helping you enter a new challenge, and above all, experience the lesson and learn from it.

CHAPTER 9

Spiritualism, I believe, is not a religion. Spiritual beliefs and findings are practices that heal the soul, make peace with the mind, strengthen the body, and calm your chakras (especially your third eye).

Spiritualism is an individual experience. Everyone has the ability to discover an equal level of opportunity to maintain the joys and wonders of their life journeys' purposes.

It's knowing and being able to acknowledge that feeling of completely understanding how it makes us feel and how we can celebrate it without holding back and how to let go of those human emotions, particularly feeling judged by others. To have the sense of who we are and what we can discover and understand about ourselves and our life journeys—the valuable knowledge of what is!

Not even the most spiritual people know everything there is to know about spiritualism; is has many facets. I believe each person's journey into the spirit world is based on that person alone. Therefore, each person will have a different level of spirit divine within himself or herself. But once shared with someone, a teaching occurs and the other person takes the same pathway. This is what I call a crossroad point.

Crossroads happen all the time and on separate levels. Facets, created by these crossroads, are moments of time and lessons to each other on higher self. This is what awakens our whole world of who we are and God, angels, and spirits.

We can always rely on these three entities. They always look out for us and guide us on the right conduit for our pathway of life.

Never give up on them, for they will never give up on you. They are by your side the whole time and never second-guess who or what you are about. They sometimes know you better than you know yourself. There's no hiding from that.

I found this beautiful passage by Útmutató a Léleknek. It describes exactly the expectations of how to answer in a tangible manner the enlightenment of spiritualism, God, and angels.

Do You Believe in Mother?

"In a mother's womb were two babies. One asked the other: "Do you believe in life after delivery?" The other replied, "Why, of course. There has to be something after delivery. Maybe we are here to prepare ourselves for what we will be later." "Nonsense" said the first. "There is no life after delivery. What kind of life would that be?" The second said, "I don't know, but there will be more light than here. Maybe we will walk with our legs and eat from our mouths. Maybe we will have other senses that we can't understand now." The first replied, "That is absurd. Walking is impossible. And eating with our mouths? Ridiculous! The umbilical cord supplies nutrition and everything we need. But the umbilical cord is so short. Life after delivery is to be logically excluded." The second insisted, "Well I think there is something and maybe it's different than it is here. Maybe we won't need this physical cord anymore." The first replied, "Nonsense. And moreover if there is life, then why has no one ever come back from there? Delivery is the end of life, and in the after-delivery there is nothing but darkness and silence and oblivion. It takes us nowhere." "Well, I don't know," said the second, "but certainly we will meet Mother and she will take care of us." The first replied "Mother? You actually believe in Mother? That's laughable. If Mother exists, then where is She now?" The second said, "She is all around us. We are surrounded by her. We are of Her. It is in Her that we live. Without Her this world would not and could not exist." Said the first: "Well I don't see Her, so it is only logical that She doesn't exist." To which the second replied, "Sometimes, when you're in silence and you focus and you really listen, you can perceive Her presence, and you can hear Her loving voice, calling down from above." - Útmutató a Léleknek"

No dogmas of the written scripts of people and churches of individuals who proclaim they serve God. They serve themselves with their riches given to them by their parishioners who suffer by the hands of those same individuals. Disgusting abusers hide behind the church and others who help them cover up their deceit, shame, and abuse with bribes. These scripts that tell of hate, persecution, discrimination, and judgement are all written by humans … not God. No, thank you! I will not be a part of that and will not regale this theory about my God. Give me spiritual belief of the highest. That I do trust with all my heart and soul.

Happiness centres your everything. Another person cannot make you these things. I believe that's the problem with a lot of people these days. They expect others or things to make them happy.

If we try to make ourselves more confident, happy, and loving through our spiritual beings, don't you think it would make things so much more enjoyable, loving, and fulfilling for couples? It's definitely difficult when one person in a couples is spiritually minded and the other is not. I find there is a shortfall for both. It saddens me that this happens all the time.

I find it rather disturbing when people go out of their way to be seen with or have an attachment to a celebrity. They spend time, effort, and money and receive only emptiness. When people find greatness in and look up to family and friends the way they look up to actors, supermodels, and those who are famous for being famous—doing nothing other than post selfies on social media—the world as we know it will be able to step to its highest self. When it comes to matters of one's own beliefs in God, angels, and spirits, there is no real trying or desperate need to want to be with them or look up to them as people to be admired and loved. It's so sad; you are only cheating yourself.

It is easier to have someone else's opinion rather than standing with your own beliefs and trusting in your own worth. So many people seem to take the easy route. They are there and always will be as this will never change.

Communication is the key to a successful relationship be that with your spouse, partner, boyfriend, girlfriend, friends, and family members. If we don't communicate, we lack honesty. With no honesty there comes imagination. Imagination becomes fear, and fear becomes real. Fear is a real emotion. We cling to it, and it clings to us. Our imagination grows, hence it feeds the fear.

This is why it's so important to speak and allow ourselves to be honest, brave, and open with those we are close to, so we can listen to each other's feelings and fears. When we acknowledge each other's feelings and fears, imagination is put to rest. You'll find the initial thought of the fear was only the start of a relationship problem.

If you struggle with words or your emotions tend to take over during important conversations, it's always good to consider writing down what you want to say or discuss. Ask your partner to do the same. You may be surprised that theirs is nothing like yours. The saying, "Men are from Mars; women are from Venus," is so true. But with the help of communication, there can be a reunited force.

Don't be mistaken that communication will fix everything. In some cases, communication is a real art form, and for some, it's too hard to bear. This needs to be addressed if it's a problem for one of you. As long as you are aware of it, there is always hope for a breakthrough. Only when it's not recognised is there a real problem. How do you think it's all going to end? Yep, in tears! If it's not working, make the change; find what works for you. Open communication is key.

Life is essentially yours to do whatever you choose to do with it. Choose carefully, but don't hold back because of fear or regret. Also, be mindful that the choices you make are reflections—marks—on your journey. They are pivotal points as the rings on the tree trunks of life. Trust your gut and your light that is within you. Pray that no one forgets you; pray that they speak of you well and can say, "I know him/her! Wow! That woman/man is an inspiration!" And last, but not at all least, that you have the same opinion about you yourself.

It's not that Complicated

If we stick to worrying about our own journeys and not about others on their journeys, we would likely be better able to see our own paths for our life lessons. We don't need the lessons from someone else's life. It's not our business.

Stop being a sticky beak, feeding off that inquisitive mindset. It doesn't serve anything, only hearsay and a twisted version of the truth. It's okay to listen to your friends about their problems and to try and help them figure out a solution. It's not okay to carry their problems or woes into conversations with other people if that person isn't there to share with them.

Making yourself available for insight into someone's fears, hopes, disappointments, dreams, dissolutions, and friendships is when it can all go south. I can't but scream out it's not complicated! Keep it to yourself! It's not your journey, and you have no business discussing others' journeys without them. Sure, it makes for good conversation, but really!

You really need to ask, "Why?"

> Why? Because you really haven't considered or valued your own journey.

> Why? Because you love to self-loathe, and someone else's journey seems far more interesting than your own.

Why? Jealously is alive and well.

Why? Because all the above is true.

Why? Because even if you denied all the above, it's still all true.

Why? Because it's not complicated. It's habit.

Do you really want to know your true self-worth and what lessons you need to learn to have your life path lived to its absolute height of meaning and substance? If yes, stop doing the above!

It's the nature of the beast—our inquisitive beast. When you get caught up in others' life journeys, you're injuring the soul and allowing deviations to take over you own life path. But we can do it. We are intelligent humans and can repress this behaviour, thereby reflecting our self-worth and letting others do the same.

I remember a time when I was about seven years old, I eavesdropped on a conversation my mother and grandmother were having about someone else. I only understood parts of the conversation, and without knowing, I embedded it deep in my brain. Then, when I felt it was the right time, I regurgitated what I really thought was true to someone else. Well, that third party went to others and repeated exactly what I had told. This person added more to the story because his or her ego would have added its two cents, and so on, and so on.

Yes, I was only a child, but if I hadn't repeated what I thought I heard, nothing would have been said. Ego doesn't have an age barrier or scruples, and children copy everything. I knew it was wrong to eavesdrop, but I couldn't help but want to listen; I felt I was going to miss out on something big. My mother even called me "Miss Big Ears," and I disliked being called that name. I think Mum called me that in the hopes I would stop this behaviour. It didn't work.

If only I'd realised and understood the spiritual world better. It isn't what I was going to miss out on about others; it's about what I was missing about my life. I would have seen I was missing important communications about myself and messages my guides were relaying to me.

My parents raised all their children to be the best possible people we can be and to help others. We are born with two hands—one to help ourselves, and the other to extend to others.

Imagine how wonderful life would be if we all decided not to repeat what we know about others' life paths! I believe the world would be a lot more harmonious and less pugnacious, and less hearsay and egos would be fed and watered. Try it, and see for yourself how it can change your life and that of others who rely on you for updates.

Everyone—even the strongest—needs support now and then. A confident smile and a loving heart are all that is requested.

CHAPTER 10

Manifestations are a true gift that everyone has the ability to do anytime and anywhere, whether on a grand scale or with a truncated output. It's there, there is no denying it. Everyone does it at least once a day. Either consciously or subconsciously, you are manifesting, sending it out to the universe and waiting for that special thing—that nugget of wisdom—to come back into the fold.

Manifestations are called other things, including prayers, wishes, shooting stars, dreams, and goals. From an early age we are taught to manifest. Some people don't even realise that is what they are doing. Let's see, the first manifestation would be on our first birthday. Our parents teach us to make a wish and blow out the candle. But don't tell anyone the wish, or it won't come true. That part was created by superstitions, however; the actual wish sequence isn't. It's the start of a manifestation to believe that if we wish hard enough and believe, what we ask for will come to fruition.

Manifestation is the ability to think of something you desperately need or want to advance wholly in this life. As children we wish for material things, and usually it is given to us by our parents or carers. Everyone is happy with the outcome. However, manifestations are to be used wisely. Be cautious of what you are asking for and for whom praying, wishing, and asking, the principles of manifesting. Your life guides will help you and provide the necessary entities you are asking for.

The most asked question in the world today is, "Can you please give me enough money to be able to provide for me and my family?" Then the most used answer is, "I'm still waiting for it."

Always be thankful and humble when asking. You must be precise when you manifest. Know exactly what it is you want or need.

I examined a client of mine who needed "his retorts." After speaking with him through a meditational state, I asked him to repeat word for word exactly what he was manifesting. He told me he expected to find a bag full of money at his front door. This was his answer to his financial problems.

Really!

Meditation continued, and discussions brought to the surface. I discovered he had missed opportunities and awesome prospects that were repeatedly presented to him. They could have made his financial problems fade away. Instead, he chose to ignore the signs and messages sent by the angels, his life guides. I explained to him that if he asked for help (money) and his life guides provided him a chance to explore the possibilities, it was up to him not to ignore them but to run with this knowledge, be grateful they listened and extended a worthy route to creating a better life through the tangible manifestation that had arrived on his doorstep.

This client still didn't believe he was his own undoing to not having the money he so desperately needed for himself and family. I told him, "Just stop! You chose not to work for it; you accepted that it had to be in the form of literal money just to be given to you. If this is the case, you might be waiting your whole life for something that may not happen. That's what your life path is all about. Yes, it's true that it does happen to others; money just seems to land in their laps. Even so, that's not your business. It doesn't matter to your life path. You need to focus on you, not what on others have."

My client then understood what he needed to do. It wasn't too late to use those prospects to his advantage. The opportunity was still knocking on his door. When opportunity knocks at your door, remember to open it, receive it, and create it!

There are five types of manifestations.

- Epiphany—a divine manifestation
- Theophany—a visible (not essentially somatic) manifestation of a deity to a human person
- Word of God—a manifestation of the mind and the will of God
- Tidal wave—a phenomenal manifestation of emotion or singularity
- Appearance—the event of coming into spectacle

When observing these five types of manifestations, I see I'm so grateful for my ability to see and talk with the spirits. This was from my manifestations, since I was young and always asking for it. My last opportunity was presented to me in Port Arthur.

It was my tidal wave, my epiphany, and my appearance (my angel), which no one else witnessed, as well as the Word of God, who answered all my prayers.

Manifestations can also be affected towards us negatively, including through worry, stress, imagination, visions, and visions of disasters. These types of manifestations work against us. Always work towards positivity no matter how dim or bleak the situation. There is no room for negativity to spoil our rewards. If you think negatives, they will certainly come to you; it's what you put out to the universe. So be careful and particular of what you ask.

CHAPTER 11

This came to me the night of the October 31, 2010. I went to bed feeling sleepy at 9:15 p.m. Then I couldn't believe it. I watched the clock go around until 2:45 a.m. I was thinking out loud; my brain wouldn't shut down. Stuff was coming out and then these words came, and analogies were bursting with cognizance. I thought, *I should be writing this down.* Then I wondered if it was thinking this or if it was my life guide telling me so. I chose to remember it in the morning. I was too tried to get up out of bed. Trust me, if the spirits need or want you to know things, it will surely happen when you least expect it.

The heading I was told to write was just that: "Words are heard." It was my life guide who spoke to me, but it was definitely a message from God. I'd been asking for his guidance and help, and he came through for me once again.

I hope that you get and are just as excited as I am about the stories I am about to tell you. They are true and shared with no embellishments. They're all facts and no holds barred. That's me—straightforward and direct with the truth. But I am compassionate when it comes to people and their feelings.

I love the knowing and being close to God and all my chosen ones and my beloved ones who have passed over. God's grace has enabled me to witness things that scare those who don't believe in the afterlife. I had hoped to be able to convince some of the people I am friends with to share in the joyous truths of God and his followers, but regrettably, it was not meant to be. This is why I chose to write this book, to spread the word that what I saw was truly remarkable and to share my proof through my photos of my angel and all the young boys who came forth for me. They heard me call out to them. As well as the German shepherd that is standing guard in front of them all.

I am truly blessed. I have my family, who is my life, and a job that is one more avenue for God to shine though via massage with my healing hands.

Still, God provides me with the insight of what to expect on the other side after passing. I still have to pinch myself sometimes. I have a wonderful life.

Sometimes

Sometimes things are better shared. Sometimes those things we put on the back burner need to be brought forward and reassessed.

At one time or another, we will get a broken heart. The thing that will mend the crack is support from family and friends.

Sometimes we get choices. It's knowing if we chose the right one.

Sometimes it's better to say nothing at all. The silence can be deafening.

Sometimes you can hear your path guide tell you to take a different direction or approach to either a person or an idea. Next time, listen! You and they have an agreement that they will help you on your quest of life.

All the family you have, all the people you meet, all the people you think about, all the people you don't think about or meet, all the people you build relationships with—whether short or lifelong—all came from contracts made with each other well before you decided when you (your soul) would enter your mother's womb. So don't be surprised when you engage that someone on your path of life. You may feel you have met that person before but can't remember where. Just remember what I told you previously.

Newborn babies are the most genius of all human beings. They have all the answers to what our life purposes should be and how we need to acquire them. Unfortunately, once born we start to forget what that is and where we were last to stay or visit. Who was the last person we spoke to? My thoughts are that God sends us off on our journeys with love and light. You see, God is the last person we talk to and see. How wonderful is that?

The next time you are fortunate enough to hold a baby, use your third eye, your intuitive strengthens, and ask the child to help you see his or her last visit with God, and try to remember the send-off he gave you.

Your life's pathway is chosen not just by you but by all who know you and are or have been a part of your life, even before they entered their mothers' womb. God is a strict disciplinarian when it comes to life paths as they are all corrective predetermined agreements.

Only your life guide can ask God if a change can be implied to your life's contract. That is because you have prayed and prayed and prayed. Ask your life's guide to help you change your lessons so you can achieve what you need to whilst you are here.

Sometimes when good long-term or short-term relationships end, you can't understand what went wrong or why you were wronged. Or maybe you were the one who decided to end the relationship. It usually ended with a reason but not generally the real reason. This is sometimes when human feelings step in and it's caused too much pain, regret, and human frustration.

It's simply because they have fulfilled their contractual agreements with you for this lifetime. It can be sad, heartbreaking, and painful. You have learned the lessons of life in which their lives affect yours.

Instead of playing the blame game or siding with or involving others who may or may not need to learn lessons in this vocation, the matter will not be resolved. Therefore, you can continue the pain and suffering, or you can wish them well on their journeys, and perhaps you'll see them at another stage of your life as planned or in the afterlife.

Trust is a two-way street. You may feel there is always an imbalance. There is one person you can trust, and that is yourself. Trust your instincts, and listen to you and your life guide. They are both on your side.

Have faith in your trust because without faith, there no conviction.

Creativity is a gift from God. How we decide what or how it develops depends on one's state of mind and prepetition of one's soul. This is why it is very important that when we have children, they should be taught to use these gifts in a manner that benefits the talented as well as the associated cohorts. Human violations are often created by an adult with only one ambition—to use and abuse his or her position. And sometimes, by a child who has been shown a corrupt passage they will have to endure for their life. (Unless it was their choice to be a part of their pathway of life.) We simply need to establish growth and fortifiable tenets in the young, so they will become more open to the idea of having a spiritual existence and become well-equipped men and women in their pursuit for their life purposes. Why is it that when we are children we can love all those who care for and love us, but once we become adults, we make judgements and become corrupt and more apt to draw assumptions about others?

Perpetual generations of humans could have a real global effect. Can you imagine what the world would be like if we just regaled the thought of our purposes in our life and not about who's got the best house or the most money?

What if our parents chose a different belief in how we were structured, and our fundamentals as human beings were altered in a more-spirited, proactive way? Spiritualism over religion. What do you think would happen?

I believe we would find ourselves with peace, freedom, and an abundant, fulfilling life. No more clouded thoughts of escapade and exploit but higher majestic love and admiration for God and reassurance for one's ability to achieve great things in this life of the now.

CHAPTER 12

It was September 29, 1987. It was a beautiful day, and I was both happy and sad. I was in hospital about to have a caesarean. My baby was a placenta Previa birth. I was in and out of hospital since I was twenty-seven weeks pregnant. For those of you who don't know of this condition, I'll explain.

In this condition, the egg attaches to the cervix rather than to the wall of the uterus, which is usual. As the foetus grows, it stretches the cervix, causing haemorrhaging. Not knowing whether the baby is going to survive can be very scary to the parents.

It was a very traumatic event in Michael and my lives. We had Leigh, who was only just sixteen months old at the time. My doctor was a godsend to me. He reassured me that he was doing his best to help the baby along.

My doctor gave me an injection to help the baby's lungs develop faster. I was to stay in hospital for complete rest. This was not as easy as it sounded. Michael had to go to work, so we relied on our families to take care of Leigh.

Our son was born five and half weeks premature. I prayed to God with the loudest voice in my mind so he could hear me. *Please, please, let my baby be all right.*

He was such a beautiful boy, weighing five pounds eight ounces. Not a bad weight for a premmie. The nurses rushed him away from me and placed him in a humidity crib. After seven long days, I could finally hold my new baby, who we named Matthew. Every day of those seven days I prayed to God that my little boy would make a full recovery.

I remember a dream I had one night in the hospital. At least I thought it was a dream. My aunty Leslie, who passed over when I was in England, came to me in my dream and said everything would be fine. She told me not worry because she would look over Matthew for me until I decided that there was no longer a need.

I know whenever Aunty Leslie is around me because I can smell her perfume, Taboo. It a gentle reminder that she is close by me. It's how she opens communications with me. Then I can sit back and visit and catch up with her. Maybe receive a message. If you sense a particular smell—such as cigars, pipe, cigarette smoke, or perfume—or maybe you hear your named called out, but when you look around nobody's there … you guessed it; spirits are trying to get your attention.

Matthew is now twenty-eight years old, and my aunty Leslie still watches over him. She does this because I still need her to do so. I worry about my children all the time. I think every mum goes through this. But it is comforting to know that I have family support on the living side as well as continuing support from my loved ones who have passed over.

I am truly grateful to God for my family and friends, and for this wonderful life.

CHAPTER 13

I decided to go back to studies after my youngest child, Jeffrey, finished year 12 in high school. It was agreed between my husband and I that when we had children, I would be a stay-at-home mum and support him in his business. I generally ran the office—answering the phone, inputting data, invoicing, doing payroll, and so on—whilst raising three children. It was the perfect situation for us.

Then 2009 came about, and the long-awaited day was upon me. I had to decide what I would like to have as a career, especially since I was forty-seven years old. Not that age is a barrier. I was anxious about going back to school.

After going online, I googled "massage therapist" and discovered the Massage Academy. This was big! I did a lot of toing and froing and finally decided this was the course for me. I'd get certificates 3 and 4 in massage and maybe diploma following.

I was very nervous and quite worried that I wouldn't be able to actually do the theory side of this course. I wasn't the best student through my academic years. School was an uphill struggle for me when it came to learning and applying something new.

I was going to do it. No more doubts. No more negative thoughts. I'm going to do it. I could hear Grandma Wilkinson whisper, "Yes! Yes!" And cheering!

First Dream

April 13, 2009, Easter Monday, was my first day of college. I had a brilliant day filled with excitement, anxiousness, and an enthusiastic sense to learn. Yes, I was meant to be there. I met some really nice women in my class. Like me, they were guided to this place. One young woman who stood out to me was named Scarlett. She was a vibrant, colourful character and always brought energy to the class. We shared lots of laughter and times of really in-depth conversations. She was intrigued by my gift. I told Scarlett of my visions and predictions about our classmates. She discussed her dreams with me and asked my thoughts as to how to interpret them. I encouraged her to accept what was happening to her as she had the gift.

Scarlett and I drove to college together each morning. Well, I drove; she didn't have her driver's licence yet and lived only five minutes away. One particular morning I told her about my previous night's dream. The classroom was furnished with long tables and swivel chairs. After about two weeks into the course, we always sat at the same place and in the same chair. It was just a given that whoever arrived first naturally had the first choice of where to sit. Victoria arrived first and then Scarlett and me followed by Richa, Dimis, and Evelyn. Then came Corbin, Liz, Nancy, Gemma, and Natalie. These last five sometimes arrived in a different order but not usually.

Getting back to the dream I was telling Scarlett about, I dreamed Corbin would be sitting in my chair. He would arrive before Scarlett and me. She laughed and said, "No way. He's always running late." Two days later, we walked into the classroom to find Corbin sitting in my chair with a smirk on his face. I didn't say anything to him. He was quite pleased with himself about sitting in my chair.

Scarlett freaked out and yelled, "OMG, it came true." I smiled and applauded myself within, choosing not to make a big deal about it. I left that to Scarlett.

Second Dream

Another dream was about Gemma. We were in the lunchroom, and she was very upset. Her eyes were red and bloodshot and tears ran down her face. She was trying to explain to me why she was crying, but I couldn't hear her as the lunchroom was noisy. I hugged her and told her that everything would be okay and not to worry.

At lunchtime that day, Scarlett tapped me on my shoulder and said, "Have a look at Gemma." I turned around to witness her crying uncontrollably. I got up and walked over to her. I asked Gemma what the problem was. She answered me, but I couldn't hear her because of the noisy lunchroom. She repeated that she was panicking about the big test. I hugged her, comforting her with my embrace and words. I told her she would be fine and not to worry. If she needed help, we would help each other. Truth be told, we all felt the same way.

Scarlett came up to me and said, "It came true again! Katie, you are a freak."

Third Dream

I dreamed Dimis was pregnant, but there were plenty of problems along the way. When I told her about the dream, Dimis mentioned she and her husband were having problems falling pregnant. She was told it was very unlikely they would have a baby. I spoke with Dimis with compassion as I, too, understood the trials and heartbreaks of trying to fall pregnant.

I saw Dimis after graduation on Tuesday, June 30, 2009. We both attended the infant massage course, Scarlett and Richa were there, too. When it came to saying goodbye to everyone, it was hugs and kisses all round. I walked up to Dimis, gave her a hug and kiss, and whispered in her ear, "Some good news next month. Let's wait and see!"

Fourth Dream

It was about our exam for college—the big exam! It was an assessment about sports massage. We had to know all the names of muscles and their functions, insertions, and origins. It was going to be tough.

The day before we had to choose partners for the test. One would be the client and the other the therapist.

I dreamed that I would be handed the gastrocnemius muscle chart and would have to explain it and its functions, and so on. The next morning, I told Scarlett of what I dreamed.

We stood at our massage tables and partnered up. The teacher had eight to twelve muscle charts in his hands. He shuffled them and chose a chart for me. But he changed his mind and handed me a different chart. Yes, you guessed it; it was the gastrocnemius chart. To Scarlett's amazement, the same muscle chart was handed to me. I turned to her and said, "I had a dream."

She just stood there with her mouth agape. "OMG, Katie!" We couldn't say much because it was an assessment, and the lecturer was with us in the exam area. Scarlett just smiled and diagnosed the problem with full, correct answers. Nailed that exam! It was then, at that very moment, I knew it was not a coincidence. This was something far greater.

After we completed the exams and were headed to the lunchroom, Scarlett announced what had happened. Out classmates weren't that surprised, especially after all the other dreams had come true.

I definitely felt different and still changing. It's hard to describe my emotions. However, I just kept saying to Grandma Wilkinson, "Bring it on! I want it all!"

On the June 19, 2009, I passed with flying colours and received my cert 4 in massage. I was so proud of myself and knew this would change my life in so any ways.

On June 21, 2009, Michael, I, and friends Joanne and Stanley took a trip to Tasmania. We spoke about it with Joanne and Stanley as they had never been before. Michael and I love going there. We all decided to take a holiday. I needed this time away to have some much-needed downtime with Michael and to take a break from everything.

We went the same time of year as before and had such a wonderful time. I hoped that this trip to Port Arthur would bear my intuitiveness with clarity. My intuition was running high. This would make for a definite pinnacle pin and transform my life.

Looking back on my experience still gives me goose bumps, and a flood of spirits surround me. I use that strength to help me through my toughest days and to shine for others who need that same strength. It's within me to help heal others as well as myself. I feel it; I know it, and I rejoice it!

CHAPTER 14

I'm a straightforward person. I need to know the why. Come to me if you have a problem, and I will show you respect. A lot of people can't handle my truths. I do show compassion and have filters for people's feelings, however, I'm a person who just needs to be honest with situations or gripes.

Sometimes that can come back and bite me. But I feel okay with that, as I am who I am. It's not for me to change others. It's up to them to change.

I'm blessed to have my gifts. They have been with me from an early age; I recall since I was about seven or eight years old. My psychic ability has been more prevalent in my life since I became a massage therapist. It's what I have always wanted and asked for.

I then realised the people I cross paths with are meant to help me on my journey, to meet the criteria and provide lessons to learn the whys and wherefores of this life's wondrous offerings. People are in your life for a reason or a season or a lifetime. You are either learning a life lesson from them or providing one for them. Don't let your emotions take over what was or what is. That's human nature, but allow the spiritual needs to overflow. This will help you adapt to the notion that this was a lesson. Don't allow it to affect who you are. Don't let it define who you were, and don't let the lesson be wasted. Accept it, and trust that the lesson will lead to a more wonderful and joyous life with many more twists and turns without devaluing the things you have as a reminder that you are living as you choose the pathways that make you happy.

I followed my dreams and became more eager to learn about the gifts God has given me, trusting me to help people and get the word out there that this is real. He trusts me to be as honest I can. I have no hidden agenda; I only want to share with anyone who wants to know the truth about the afterlife, how to be the best human being you can possibly be, and to learn the lessons we need to achieve whilst we are here on earth. The ability to be more open and to take the initiative with spiritualism will help you have the optimism and confidence to be able to walk in the pathway with light and love in your heart and soul.

Once I began spreading the word that I was a fully qualified massage therapist, I started to work straightaway. Michael is such a love; he built two rooms for me underneath his office and work unit at his place of business. It was perfect. I decorated it and placed important pieces such as crystals and mementos in my domain. It was my special place, where I would feel my spirituality shine through and be connected with my God, angels, and all who walked in either living or passed.

I announced to my clientele that I was now offering readings, meditation sessions, and healing. Soon, many clients wanted more and more of this service. I was in my element doing what I do best. —massage, psychic readings, and both together. Very happy clients gave out recommendations, and my clientele list grew and grew. There were exciting times ahead with wonderful people to meet and heal. This certainly was—and is—a true calling for me.

I loved my work, meeting different people. I knew I could use the power of my healing hands on them. I discovered I could tell them where they were in pain, which was not usually where they said they were hurting. My clients couldn't believe that I had the ability to scan their bodies with my hands and feel where the problem was. When they asked, "How do you do that?" I always told them it was a special gift. I had many return clients and new clients from referrals. It was going great.

Remember in chapter 4 I mentioned timing? You see, it was the right time for me with everything that had happened in my life up to that time. Especially when I had the fortunate meeting with a woman named Maria.

Maria advertised in the local newspaper about a workshop on how to develop one's psychic ability. I thought, *this is a must. I need to know how to use my psychic ability in a more constructive manner,* I was ready to explore new opportunities in this area. Wow, I was hooked! I had amazing results with these beautiful souls. Maria is a reverent and also has her own spiritual church. I now had a place I could count on if I needed a backup for any questions regarding spiritualism. My church is in my heart, mind, and soul.

I learnt spirituality means tolerance, honesty, unconditional love, understanding, empathy, forgiveness, awareness of self, integrity, awareness of others, patience, kindness, generosity of spirit, and compassion to me.

Once you believe that you have all those qualities within you and it should feel natural.

Follow these steps:

Balance: law of cause and effect.

Karmic: law of what goes out you will get back.

Akashic records: manifesting demystified; to deepen your understanding of yourself.

Reading your own Akashic records is not principally problematic, but there are some fundamentals. One is the ability to get into a meditative state. You need to be able to set aside your current thoughts and be open to whatever information you may find. I am a spirit with a physical body, not a physical body with a spirit. The spirit does not change. Thoughts are living things; as you think so it is. You are what you think, not what you think you are. Now you can better understand déjà vu. If you remember a person, thing, or place, then yes, you are undergoing an out-of-body experience. Embrace that data to the best of your ability as this is a message, a gift for you, and a lesson.

This little prayer is the one I use to help protect me. I want to share it with you.

Prayer for Protection

In the name of Jesus Christ, I call upon the spirits of light to stand guard at the doorway of my soul to guide me in the ways of truth, love, and light to protect me against the forces of darkness and deception. Amen.

This verse I use as a cleanse technique before I give a reading or massage.

Cleanse Technique

(Say out loud)

In the name of God, I cleanse my body. (Using your middle two fingers of your right hand, gently rub your third eye in a clockwise motion 3 times and then use both hands to wash over both cheeks of your face simultaneously). Flick your wrists and hands to let go of any bad energies that are attached to you.

I cleanse my soul (both hands cupped together and wash over face, over the top of your head, and down past the back of your neck). Flick your wrists and hands to let go of any bad energies that are attached to you.

Repeat from the start until you feel cleansed. You will know when it is done.

Psychometry is used for readings with objects. This is a useful tool. However, I'm best at a reading visually and audibly when providing a massage or meditation for my clients. Using chakra awareness, the body's seven energy centres, and in your hands and feet, I can tap into the person's emotions, functions, life force, vitalities, and unification of the higher self. All remarkable facts to help extract what spirits will reveal to me, so I can be the best possible messenger with love and light.

An aura is an egg-shaped electric field that surrounds us. It reflects everything we think and feel as well as our moods and health. There are many colours in the aura. These colours swirl and change depending on the things previously mentioned. Once cleansed, the aura is filled with positive energy.

Every living thing has an aura around its outer edge. The shape or glow is commonly known as the life force. The life force appears as a white light and varies in size from a half inch to four inches, depending on your state of being at the time. The aura appears at the moment of physical birth and remains until three days before physical death, when it begins to fade regardless of how death occurs.

When my clients ask to receive a meditation, I ask the spirits to provide a personal meditation for me to write down and then help my clients meditate. I have received so many from spirits. They are a beautiful, personal footbridge to your spirit guides and astral travel.

Everyone needs to do astral travel on a regular basis. It usually happens in a sleep state but can also happen while daydreaming or meditating. It occurs when the spirit moves away from the physical body. The physical body and the spirit are connected by a silver cord, which is limitless. No one can get lost during astral travel as the spirit will always return to the physical body. Only when physical death occurs is the silver cord is severed, and the spirit and the silver cord return to the spirit realm.

Always treat spirits with respect. When asking questions, it's always one question, one answer. Accept what you receive until or unless it is proven otherwise.

I was on my way to the full extent of psychic readings and providing meditations and crystal massages to balance the body, mind, and soul. I have it all! Yes, God had answered all my wishes and prayers. I'm truly blessed.

There's something else that will astonish you. You just need to be in an awareness state. If you see a feather floating down from the sky out of nowhere, or it could be there at your feet, don't ignore this communication. It's from an angel, sending you love and light and letting you know it has heard your prayers and heard you ask for help.

Have you ever wondered how many birds there are in the world? Well, how about your country? Well, how about your state? What about your suburb? Even if I took a guess about the number in my suburb, I would say 20,000 birds. That's just at a guess; it's probably more. Okay, 20,000 birds in my suburb. My question is where are all their dropped feathers? Birds lose feathers, so where are they all? That's a lot of feathers. My point is you should come across at least ten feathers a day if that is the case. Don't you think? However, I can truly say I just don't see them. My next point is when you do see a white feather you will know who it's from. It's a message—a calling card—left by angels to let you know they are there for you. Ask for their help and guidance.

CHAPTER 15

My grandma passed away on February 22, 2014. Grandma Kennedy was a wonderful woman. She was two months' shy of her ninety-fourth birthday.

We were always close as she dedicated her life to family. She and Grandad had nine children, eight sons and one daughter. They were all loved and wanted. Never did I hear my grandma raise her voice or have a bad thing to say to us kids. She was definitely a saint to raise all these kids and then grandchildren, great-grandchildren, and great-great grandchildren. She was always a hands-on grandparent, helping out wherever she could without complaining or making a fuss. She was always glad to see you. We used to get a bit of a guilt trip if we hadn't seen her for a while. She would say, "I haven't seen you for ages," when it had only been a couple of weeks. But for her, it felt like a couple of months.

One of my most favourite memories of my grandma was when she taught my sisters and me to bake when I was young. It was such an enjoyable occurrence. She baked all sorts of delicious puddings and cakes. There was always leftover pastry for us girls to make our own rollie pollie. We spread jam over our rolled out pastry and then rolled it into a long bun. It baked in the oven until golden brown. It was so delicious. When I think back to those days, I always remember, too, that Grandma made sure she praised us for doing such a great job.

We lost Grandad Kennedy from a heart attack about twenty years ago now. He is missed every day. Grandad would visit me particularly in my sleep and dreams. He gave me messages and led me in ways of how to better my spiritual meanings. I thank him for that. He wishes he'd been more in tune with his body and made more of an effort to look after his health. He honestly thought he would have a longer life.

As the years passed, Grandma developed more health issues and conditions than you could poke a stick at. By age ninety-two, she had diabetes, which made her legs discolour from lack of circulation. I told Grandma, "Come and see me in my clinic. I will massage your legs and hands." We had a great time during that hour we spent together at my clinic every week. Her legs did change. She was excited as she hated the dark brown areas and uneven tones on both legs. During this time, we talked about my younger years, laughed, and shared stories.

Adults in the Kennedy family always protected their young, so as children, we lived in a world where love, laughter, hugs, and kisses were in abundance. Yes, I was very fortunate to be raised by loving parents, grandparents, aunts, and uncles.

One day during her visit to my clinic, Grandma spoke about death. She told me that she was actually scared of death. It was then I disclosed my gifts to her. I also told her what I experienced and that I was able to speak to spirits. She was overwhelmed with excitement and wanted to know about it all.

I told her everything would be okay when the day came that she would be called on to leave the earth and her family. Every week Grandma was always eager to learn more about the afterlife. We promised each other that she would come to me. I was cheeky in asking her to come to me as I see her with my eyes and not the third eye. About 2:00 a.m. on Tuesday, Grandma's sister, Aunty Jean, came to me with a poem for Grandma. I wrote it down, took it with me to the hospital, and read it to her. She loved it, and we had an eye-to-eye connection right there. She knew it would be soon.

Grandma told me she no longer feared death and was grateful for every day she lived. I told her she still had lessons to learn. Weeks turned into months, and after several months of her coming to see me at the clinic, we had to stop. Grandma had a dreadful fall and was in and out of hospital for months. The last time she went into hospital, she never came out. The last week of her life I had the privilege of sitting by her bedside, holding her hand and talking with her about moving towards the white light. She kept asking me, "When am I going to leave this world?" She had enough. Her body function wasn't the same, and her dignity was slowly depleting.

The day before she passed away, I decided I no longer needed to be with her; she was ready to leave this earth. I kissed her and told her I loved her and that she was the best grandma a girl could ever wish for. I thanked her for being a wonderful role model. She told me she loved me, too, and that I had been a wonderful granddaughter. The next day, I received a phone call from my dad, telling me that my grandma, his mother, was gone. I was upset at the thought I'd never get to hug or kiss her again. But my gifts would enable me to still communicate with her.

Communication happened within days. Grandma came to me and asked me to write down a message in the form of a poem for each of her children. I agreed to do this and happy to pass these messages on to them. It took exactly one month. All nine poems where executed and handed to those persons except for one. I gave that one to a brother Grandma had chosen to be the bearer of the message. He would deliver the message when he felt it was right and try to explain the how and why of the message. Otherwise, I don't think he would have been believed it to really be a message from Grandma.

Grandma kept her word to me about channelling through me and using my gifts to share with her family and to leave an everlasting message beyond the passing over to the afterlife. What a gift it was though some days I was very drained and upset, especially when doing the poems.

Sharing her messages of love, awareness of her own children, dreams for them, adoring love toward them, and her everlasting journey as a mother even after death was an extraordinary experience and an inspirational event. It is a privilege to be able to say that I was the one she chose to share her words and feelings towards her children. This was a moment in my life I shall cherish and never forget.

It doesn't matter how old you are or what beliefs you may have. It's the purpose of the you who are gifted to share whenever you can, even if people judge you and probably think you're crazy. As I have learnt, most people who have come across my path are more than happy to hear about any type of intuitiveness or message from a passed loved one. Use the guidance provided by the angels and life guides to gauge your contribution and to restrain you when needed. That gut instinct will never fail you.

This is the message Grandma sent to me after her passing. This was on April 22, 2014, exactly two months from the day she died.

Gifts to Katie

Jesus has come forth as far and wide to reach out to you and
touch your heart, giving you the answers you so dearly ask.

The answers are all around you now; looking for them is the hardest part.

Sometimes look where you don't see, and there
the answer will be within thee.

Trust in my words, my child, to change the
world with your guided hope.

Bend with knee and pray with your soul, and
there you will receive answers untold.

Now go forward and use the knowledge of the
mighty gifts that you have been given.

Struggles and triumphs are one's life joys, and there you will
carry the load of believers and the ones who stand alone.

Trust more in yourself, and take what is yours; there you will be
contented with love in your soul. More love that is possible, for
you are truly blessed. Never lose sight of the challenging quest.

Now I shall leave you alone for a quiet time now, but still keeping
my eye on you … need only call my name, and I shall be there to
listen to your heart … and never forget your grandmother's love.

Grandma

CHAPTER 16

After everything, it still amazes me when people come into my life and at that moment, I can make a remarkable evaluation about their lives. I just blurt it out; I can't seem to hold back. The spirits like to push me, especially when they feel the need to get someone's attention.

When I let someone whose loved one passed over about that person, he or she would often remark that it was that person's birthday yesterday or it was an anniversary or something special had presented itself. Then I had people say, "Yes, I have been struggling lately," and I would be able to relay a message of hope and reinforce that their loved ones are watching over them. I can let those who weren't fortunate enough to be able to say goodbye or to have told someone they loved him or her and how special they were to them know their loved ones know how they felt.

This happens all the time. For example, I run a community site on social media as a volunteer service—you know, giving back, something everyone should do at least once in their life. Mary runs a similar site, and late one night she sent me a private message, telling me to be wary about a certain member within her group who was being dishonest and so on. She thought this person might in my group.

Just at that moment, a spirit came forth, a male energy who was very worried and desperately trying to seek his sister. This energy told me how he passed away when he was young. He kept asking me to write to Mary and ask her if she have a brother who passed. I kept telling him that I didn't know this woman personally; we only sometimes corresponded via the two groups. If I wrote to her with personal questions, it would look like I'm a crazy person. He assured me that Mary would embrace this moment and had been waiting for this sign. I told him okay because he wasn't leaving until I made contact with her on his behalf.

So, I wrote to Mary. "Can I ask you a personal question? Firstly, do you believe in the spiritual world?"

Mary wrote back, "Oh, yes, I do, Hun. Why?"

Me: "Do you know I'm a professional psychic?"

Mary: "Really? Wow. Are you picking something up about me?"

Me: "Do you have a brother?"

Mary: "OMG, yes!"

Me: "Has he passed?"

Mary: "Oh shit. Now I'm shaking. Yes, he has!"

Me: "He is here with me now."

Mary: "Oh, is he, my darling little bro?"

Me: "He was in a vehicle accident, and he was very young."

Mary: "Motorbike, and yes, he was young. He was only twenty-three."

Me: "Letting you know that he is with his family and that he is fine, and your grandparents. He sends this message to you. A message of hope to you … 'Keep up your fight against the odds.' It will come to make sense very soon. Love and light they will always send and watch over you. Cheers, Mary. Thanks for letting me get that out."

Mary: True. "I'm fighting to lose weight as I need a double lung transplant as I have a very rare lung condition that is fatal."

Me: "Well, now I know why your little brother contacted me. I'm a massage therapist, and I'm offering you a massage therapy session using warmed crystals. It will balance your chakras, relieve your stress levels, and allow in light and clarity."

Mary: "That sounds wonderful, but we are on a one-wage income at the moment, and I can't really afford it."

Me: "Don't you worry about that; this will be free to you. I'm more than happy to give you this as therapy. I understand why your brother was insisting I make contact with you."

Mary: "Katie, I cannot thank you enough for your kindness and for letting me know about my little brother. I miss him dearly. I'm sorry he had to come and bug you. But I say that everything happens for a reason. Xxx"

As you can see from this experience with Mary, it's not in my control. The spirit used my ability to help loved ones in need of their help and guidance. As for Mary's brother, he often comes through and listens to my thoughts as he finds himself with the same opinions and thoughts as I do, and he once did. He tells me what he misses the most, apart from his family, are his thoughts and how he had the freedom to think and feel about anything and everything. Then the next day, he could change his mind or learn something new and share that knowledge with whoever would listen. Now he is paving the way to be reborn again. This time he has decided he needs to learn how to strive for better knowledge of the spiritual heart and send a vibrant light to those he will touch through the channels of life and meet along the way.

… … … … … … … … … …

I also met Portia through social media. She is a single mum of three who suffers from mental health issues. However, through my words and spiritual connections, I have been able to help her. She is a lovely person and always has good intentions. Portia wants to get more out of life and to be able to give her children the same. This is some of what transpired.

Me: "That's the disease what talks of death. Whenever you feel that way, talk to me anytime, day or night. It repels off me. This is thing right! You don't even need to say that you are having a bad day.

"You can keep that to yourself. Really, the disease wishes and prays that you don't talk to me. This is how it can do its worst. Keeping me from you is its target. So we are better armed now. No excuses, right! You have already won, Portia. Now the disease is really pissed off. It will try again. Like I said, text me, call me to chat."

Portia: "Makes a lot of sense as I can't talk to anyone when I'm down and don't like telling anyone it's a mental problem. I just went deep into bipolar and didn't move or talk for a week or so. I loved reading what you just wrote. This makes me want to start to fight. I didn't have your number before but have it now. Thank you for that. I totally get it."

Me: "Great. Now get out there, and start living your life in a new day. And count your three blessings. No one person can change their life if they don't make the change."

… … … … … … … … … …

Ruby—October 28, 2009

Ruby is a massage client of mine. When I first start off the massage, some clients like to chat through it. At the start of anyone's massage, I let the client know where I feel their pain after scanning their bodies with my open hands that hover over them. Ruby said to me, "Katie, I just don't know how you do that, detecting pain by just gliding your hands over my body."

I replied, "It's a gift. She giggled, and I told her, "No, seriously. It's a gift."

Ruby replied, "I'm intrigued."

"I'm psychic. Would you like to know more?"

"Yes. I love all that stuff. I'm really open to that type of thing."

I told her briefly about my angel from Port Arthur who showed herself to me and that I see things in my mind's eye. I had discovered that when I saw pictures in black and white, they were things in the past. As for coloured pictures, they were about things in the future.

I progressed with her massage in silence. As I started to massage her right leg, I mentioned in a soft voice, "You have major pain running down your leg that ends at the tibia."

"Can you tell me how I did it?"

"Yes. I can see you climbing very steep stairs [concrete steps] and one handrail going up from a basement. You are struggling in heels up these stairs."

"Oh my, yes. I park in the city in a basement. I have to wear heels as part of my uniform, and I do struggle to climb these stairs every day of the week."

I had another vision of her. "I also see you climbing a steep driveway leading to a backdoor entrance, walking in, and you have a surprise. You are extremely happy to share news with your family."

"Oh my goodness! I was at my mum's place before I came to you. She does have a very steep driveway, and I did go to the backdoor entrance, and I did get a surprise."

"Really?"

"Yes. Mum made my favourite chocolate slice."

"Chocolate slice?"

"Yes, I love chocolate slice."

I don't think you were that happy about chocolate slice!"

"Oh yes. I just love it."

"I do feel it's something else."

When Ruby came in for her massage the next week, she walked through the doorway to my clinic rooms, stood at the table, and announced she was pregnant. "How wonderful and exciting for you. But knowing this information, I can't massage you until you are twelve weeks or over." And yes, Ruby did confide to me that the surprise she had told her mum about was, in fact, that she was pregnant. But she still thinks that chocolate slice is pretty special, too.

There are so many more stories of people who have crossed my pathway. Too many to put into this book.

Run with Your Eyes Shut

Run with your eyes shut but your mind open. Things will unbalance you; trust your balance as this will heighten you to great levels.

Run with your heart free but your desire tight-fisted. Memories will bring you back and forth; remember the memories and lessons that you learnt will bring you to a point of contentment and happiness.

Run with your soul but your free will contained. Freedom of the soul will lead you to trust and the higher of one's self.

Run with your intuition but hold no ego. Pure as white light will be your cover and protector, sheltered by guidance and one's teacher.

Run with your body, but move with your legs until they are weak, a hard-working effort your journey hasn't ended.

Run with your feelings; it's a new beginning of who you are. Do not be that person who looks behind instead of forward.

Run with your tears, but clarity is a must. Dry them first. I shall not shed; cloudy vision impedes the spirit.

Run with open hands. Catch every whisper or word. Let knowledge drive you. Let it reach out with caring, kind strokes. These will carry you to lighten the load.

CHAPTER 17

Just imagine all the senses that we have as humans—touch, smell, taste, hearing, vision. These are the only things that separate us from the living flesh. We rely on these possessions to feel, experience, and to serve as a reliable source as to what we can see. This is backed up by what we touch or smell, and so on. Take pain, for example. If we cut ourselves, we sometimes don't feel the pain until we see the blood or cut. The body is such a magnificent machine.

The spiritual manifestation within the body relies heavily on the fact you're not going to be able to see the same thing over and over again. I see it as an independent state of mind and body. This works great because restrictions are only there because we allow them to be. When we leave our bodies when we die, we lose most of our senses. We won't have the ability to taste, smell, or touch. But we will be blessed not to lose our ability to hear or see. That stays with us forever and connected with that one soul. Our ability to hear is one of the oldest senses known to humankind and the afterlife, yet humans struggle with it during their earthly lives. Some people battle to listen as well as use their voices. Yes, I know that speech is not a sense but is an art form. Doing both is unidentifiable to some at times.

We all need to try to better ourselves, learn from our teachers, and listen to wise people, mentors, and so on. Find help where we can to make us better equipped for the future generations and for the betterment of one's self to continue on after this lifetime and bring it into the next life when you chose to come back. Envision yourself as only able to listen and to speak in separate circumstances. Then envision the ability to use them together when needed. Extraordinary skills and knowledgeable people would be needed.

Can you imagine not being able to use these natural abilities? These are things we depend on all our lives. Think about it. What if we were never be able to touch, hug, comfort, please, make sound/music, applaud, feel the grass under your feet or the sand between your toes, lift a child to cuddle, hold your head close to your loved one's chest, feel the heartbeat, pat your pet, or doing outdoor activities such as gardening, fishing, and sports. The list is endless. Touch is a huge part of our being. So are smell and taste. They are enormous parts of our being. They guide us, make demands on us, speak to us, and react to us. They will be missed most when we have passed over. Don't pass up the opportunity to stop and smell a flower, the seawater, a newborn baby, a bakery, freshly cut grass, eucalyptus trees. I know it's a cliché, but be grateful for those unique treasures. Accept gifts from nature and those made from humans because they stay on earth with your body. You will only have fond memories of them, so make sure you have them well embedded in your psyche. As the saying goes, "You can't take it with you!" Well, not material items, but you will always have your memories. This is why I say to enjoy your senses and emotions. Live life and live it well. Snippets of precious cargo will replay over and over again when disembarking this earth. You will be glad you took advantage and can share this splendid epic movie about one's self.

CHAPTER 18

Photograghs taken at Port Arthur, Tasmania by Katie E Beryl

This photo was taken at Port Arthur in the dissection room. This is a ghost light, bursting with energy and light. Can you see the face coming through at the right of the picture? It is definitely in front of me but behind the guy at the doorway. You can see it was in front of the wooden door jam. The spirit was trying to make contact with me.

This was taken in the main prison at Port Arthur. See the orbs floating in the walkway? Do you see the entity in the centre of the walkway? This was a very unsettled entity. It appears in the photo as a brown tinge. It crept around me, trying to get me out of this place. The rectangular white block appeared in the photo but there wasn't anything there.

This photo was taken in the main prison cells at Port Arthur. It's the same as the previous photo, but this time, I could only see this ghost light (at the right side of the photo), flying around, very active, and full of energy.

This photo was taken on the grounds at Port Arthur. We stopped to hear the tour guide tell us of the fate of some of the prisoners at that time in Port Arthur. Do you see all the small orbs floating around? Take a look at the next photo.

This photo was taken directly after the previous photograph– (only seconds afterwards).

Do you see the ectoplasm surrounding me? Can you see how it moved towards me? It was thinner and then got thicker. There was no breeze or movement that night. There was nobody smoking, either. It was absolutely ectoplasm.

Do you see all the small bright, white Orbs?

This was taken in the main prison at Port Arthur. Once again, see the orbs and the ectoplasm? It was directly in front of me, following me on the tour.

8A 3-part photo- movement in 3 separate photographs

This was taken outside the main housing of the dissection room at Port Arthur. These three photos were taken one after the other, only seconds apart. The orbs and ectoplasm are still following me.

This was taken at Port Arthur on Dead Man's Island. Here lies James Forbes. Do you see the orbs that surround his headstone?

A Special Mention

On this day, whilst writing this book that I had presumably finished, it was brought to my attention by my spirits that I neglected to mention a person who has been in my life since I came into this world. This person is a loved one, a big sister, a confidant, and a mentor. She has always had my back.

She keeps me grounded. I never have to worry or feel there is ever a time she doesn't know that I love her deeply, and she means the world to me.

This woman has given me courage, been my cheering squad, and seen my flaws. We have been a part of each other's life journey. It gives me the greatest pleasure to announce to the world she is my aunty—my dad's sister—who my children affectionately call Aunty Leelee.

If I have learned anything from this special woman, it is you can have love and support from your family anytime, anywhere, and always! We as a family empower each other, whether female or male. Each of us has our own journeys, and yes, that is what I have mentioned throughout this book. But to be inspired and courageous is a character trait in the Kennedy family. She is certainly an inspirational person.

It's times like this when I need to reflect and be appreciative of all who help me along the way. My backup, my true, captured witness of the person I really am, and she loves me for who I am. Once again, how fortunate am I?

So many members of my family encourage me, believe in me, laugh with me, and above all, love me. Unconditional love is something everyone should strive to give. It's an amazing feeling, and I need to celebrate the fact that I have these unbelievable people in my life. My family, my incredible grandparents (both Kennedy and Wilkinson), parents, siblings, aunts, uncles, cousins, nephews and nieces. And certainly not the last nor the least, my own amazing family: my husband, Michael, who is my rock; our three children for whom words escape me and who are pure joy; and best of all are our closest friends. Unconditional love at its finest!

The last word is just the last word. There is no right or wrong ... only the last word.

BIBLIOGRAPHY

Útmutató a Léleknek, "Do You Believe in Mother?"

http://www.goodreads.com/quotes/6956846-in-a-mother-s-womb-were-two-babies-one-asked-the

NOTES

Printed in the United States
By Bookmasters